Original title:
Where Dreams Begin

Author: Gideon Shaw
ISBN HARDBACK: 978-9916-90-010-9
ISBN PAPERBACK: 978-9916-90-011-6

A Tapestry of Wishes

In the loom of stars at night,
Dreams are woven, pure and bright.
Each desire a shimmering thread,
Stitched with hopes where hearts are led.

Colors blend in patterns wide,
Radiant futures, side by side.
A fabric strong, yet soft as dew,
Wishes crafted, old and new.

The Crossroads of Hope

At the junction where paths meet,
Choices linger, bittersweet.
With each turn, a tale unfolds,
Whispers of the brave and bold.

Sunrise paints the sky with dreams,
Illuminates our silent screams.
Every step an endless chance,
To embrace the world's grand dance.

A Symphony of Beginnings

Notes arise with morning light,
Melodies take graceful flight.
Every heartbeat plays its song,
Welcoming the new and strong.

In each chord, a tale awakes,
Harmony in all it takes.
With every pause, the silence swells,
A story told where magic dwells.

Threads of Imagination

In the garden of the mind,
Ideas bloom, unique and kind.
Each thought a petal's gentle sway,
Crafting worlds where dreams can play.

Woven in a tapestry,
Of wonders wild, wild and free.
Let the colors intertwine,
In this realm, your heart will shine.

Celestial Gateways

Stars align in whispered grace,
Galaxies spin, a silent trace.
Light cascades from realms above,
Echoing the pulse of love.

Portals glow with visions bright,
Bringing dreams to heart's delight.
Silver beams and golden rays,
Guide the soul through night and haze.

Moments of Illumination

A spark ignites in quiet thought,
Wisdom blooms in battles fought.
Shadows yield to softening light,
Illusions fade, revealing sight.

Every heartbeat, truth unveiled,
In the silence, fear curtailed.
Moments pure, like morning dew,
Shimmering with vibrant hue.

In the Heart of Possibility

Within the breath of endless dreams,
Hope unfurls, or so it seems.
Roots stretch deep, as branches sway,
In the heart where wishes play.

Boundless skies and open fields,
All nature's charm, the spirit yields.
Every step a chance to grow,
In the heart, all things can flow.

A Fable of New Beginnings

From ashes rise, a phoenix bold,
Stories whispered, tales retold.
Every ending births a spark,
Lighting paths amidst the dark.

Seeds of change in soil, once bare,
Spring to life with tender care.
In each dawn, a canvas wide,
Fables dance, with hope their guide.

The Birthplace of Wonder

In the cradle of dawn's soft light,
Dreams awaken, taking flight.
Whispers of magic fill the air,
Every moment, a treasure rare.

Nature's canvas, colors bright,
Sparks of joy in pure delight.
Curious hearts begin to roam,
Finding solace in the unknown.

Unfolding through Time

A tapestry woven, thread by thread,
Each moment a journey, where we're led.
Footprints linger on paths we tread,
Stories whispered, silently spread.

The clock ticks softly in the night,
Memories shimmer, reflecting light.
Time unfolds like petals in bloom,
Embracing shadows, lifting gloom.

Ethereal Echoes

Voices of ages, softly sing,
Carried on gentle winds of spring.
Mysteries dance in the twilight air,
Ethereal echoes, everywhere.

Stars of silver, secrets told,
In the silence, stories unfold.
Connected by threads of fate,
In the night, we contemplate.

The Serenity of Hope

In the dawn of a brand new morn,
Hope arises, fragile yet sworn.
Gentle whispers of what's to be,
In every heart, a symphony.

Through storms that rattle, winds that sigh,
The light of hope will never die.
A beacon bright, it guides us near,
Filling our souls, casting out fear.

Glances of Gossamer

In twilight's soft embrace we meet,
The whispers weave a tale discreet.
With glances caught like fleeting light,
In silken shadows, love takes flight.

Beneath the moon's enchanted gaze,
Our hopes alight in tender rays.
Each moment held in fragile hands,
A dance of fate, as time expands.

The world transformed in quiet dreams,
Where nothing's ever as it seems.
With gossamer threads that intertwine,
Your heart with mine, a love divine.

As dawn awakens, colors burst,
Through fragrant petals, love's rehearsed.
In the light of day we find our way,
A glimmering path, come what may.

The Constellation of Wishes

In the tapestry of stars aglow,
Every wish takes flight, a quiet flow.
Scattered dreams like seeds in night,
Sparkling hopes twinkle in their height.

Across the heavens, stories unfold,
Whispered secrets in silver and gold.
Each heartbeat echoes with desire,
As constellations weave dreams higher.

We gather stardust, our hearts aligned,
In the universe's embrace, intertwined.
With every wish upon night's dome,
We find our way, forever home.

The cosmos sings in harmonies bright,
With each wish born from love's pure light.
Together we navigate the night,
A constellation of pure delight.

Dance of the Unborn

In a realm where shadows play,
The dance of dreams begins its sway.
Unseen futures, soft and bright,
Whispered wishes take to flight.

Ghostly figures twirl and weave,
In the silence, hearts believe.
The unborn dreams in moonlit haze,
Awake to life in tender ways.

With each fleeting step, we yearn,
For the moments yet to turn.
In rhythm's pulse, we feel the spark,
A luminous light against the dark.

In this dance, we find our song,
A symphony where all belong.
With every heartbeat, futures born,
In shadows' waltz, we greet the dawn.

Wings of a New Dawn

In the hush of the morning light,
Gentle whispers take their flight.
Breaking chains from yesterday,
Hope ascends in warm array.

Colors blend in soft embrace,
Awakening a tranquil space.
Dreams like rivers start to flow,
With each beat, the new winds blow.

Paths unknown lie yet ahead,
With courage, we are gently led.
Wings unfurl to kiss the skies,
In the dawn, our spirits rise.

The Pulse of Envisioned Realities

In the heart where visions dwell,
Time weaves stories it can tell.
Threads of thought in colors bright,
Illuminate the dark of night.

Possibilities take their form,
While dreams chase the distant storm.
With each heartbeat, truths align,
In this realm, all paths entwine.

Every choice paints futures vast,
Echoes of a vibrant past.
In this dance, we find our place,
The pulse of life, a warm embrace.

Embracing the Unknown

Step by step into the haze,
Find the beauty in the maze.
Questions rise like morning mist,
In the quiet, paths persist.

Courage glimmers in the dark,
With each heartbeat, we find spark.
Hands extended, hopes secure,
In the unknown, we endure.

Stars will guide us on our way,
Through the night and into day.
Embracing what we cannot see,
In the mystery, we are free.

Frontiers of Hope

Across the fields of endless dreams,
Shining bright like distant beams.
Each horizon calls our name,
In the journey, we find flame.

Mountains rise against the sky,
Whispers of the brave nearby.
With each step, we carve our fate,
In the hands of time, we wait.

Voices echo in the night,
Frontiers bloom in radiant light.
With a heart that dares to roam,
In hope's embrace, we build our home.

Horizons of the Mind

In the stillness, thoughts take flight,
As shadows dance in the soft twilight.
Dreams unravel, weaving the thread,
Horizons beckon where fears are shed.

Across the canvas of stars above,
Ideas glimmer like whispers of love.
With every heartbeat, new paths we seek,
In the silence, the soul learns to speak.

Reflections in the Dreamscape

In the depths of night, visions awake,
Rippling rivers, the dreams we make.
Mirrored echoes of who we are,
Shimmering softly like a distant star.

Floating gently in twilight's embrace,
Each thought a petal, time cannot trace.
Within the tapestry, truths intertwine,
Guiding the heart to places divine.

Serene Landing of Ideas

Through the clouds, ideas descend,
Gentle whispers in the mind they send.
Floating softly on a breeze so light,
Each thought a beacon, a spark of light.

Resting like feathers upon the ground,
In still moments, new worlds abound.
Nature's canvas, where visions bloom,
Inviting us to dispel the gloom.

A Canvas of Visions

Colors swirling in the dawn's embrace,
A canvas waiting for dreams to trace.
With every stroke, a story unfolds,
In the heart of creation, courage holds.

Brush of the brave, sculpting the air,
With every vision, life becomes rare.
In the silence, let inspiration sing,
On the canvas of hopes, we take wing.

Pathways of the Heart

Winding trails beneath the trees,
Whispers carried on soft breeze.
Steps that echo in the night,
Guiding souls toward the light.

With each turn, a secret shared,
Paths laid out and hearts bared.
Silent hopes and dreams unfold,
Stories woven, countless told.

Moments linger, sweet and rare,
Follow where the heart may dare.
In the dusk, our shadows blend,
On these pathways, we transcend.

Underneath Moonlit Canopies

Stars above in velvet skies,
Illuminate our whispered sighs.
Beneath the boughs, dreams intertwine,
In the glow, our souls align.

Gentle rustle of the leaves,
Crafting tales the heart believes.
Silhouettes of love in bloom,
Fragrant flowers chase the gloom.

As the night begins to fade,
In this magic, unafraid.
Underneath the watchful moon,
We find rhythms, sweet as tunes.

The Start of Something Beautiful

In the morning light it gleams,
Hope that dances, bright as dreams.
Every touch, a spark ignites,
Leading hearts to wondrous heights.

Like a canvas, fresh and new,
Painting love in every hue.
Gentle laughter, soft and clear,
In this moment, I draw near.

Brimming with potential's grace,
Hands entwined, we find our place.
With each step, we're finding ways,
To cultivate these golden days.

Chasing Twilight Shadows

As the sun dips, colors blend,
Twilight whispers, day must end.
Chasing silhouettes on the run,
In this dance, we are as one.

Fleeting glimpses, fleeting light,
Fragments captured in the night.
Every shadow tells a tale,
In the quiet, love prevails.

Mist and memories entwine,
Underneath the stars that shine.
Together we let twilight flow,
In the dusk, our spirits glow.

Maps of the Heart

In the silence, whispers wane,
Tracing veins of joy and pain.
Each line drawn by hands unseen,
In the folds where love has been.

Every curve a tale to weave,
Secrets held, we dare believe.
With each map, a journey starts,
Charting out our fragile hearts.

Through valleys deep and mountains high,
Guided by the stars on high.
In the dark, we find a spark,
Lighting up the maps we mark.

So let us roam, hand in hand,
In this world we understand.
For every path that we create,
Leads to love, we navigate.

The Elixir of Aspiration

A potion brewed from dreams and time,
In every drop, the pulse of rhyme.
From hopeful hearts, the visions flow,
An elixir sweet, that makes us grow.

With each sip, we claim our fate,
Unraveling what we create.
Bravely we chase the distant light,
With courage drawn, we take to flight.

In every sunrise, new beginnings,
With each challenge, find our winnings.
The taste of triumph, fierce and bold,
In every story waiting to be told.

So raise your glass to what will be,
In every dream, you'll find the key.
Together we'll write the firmament,
With aspirations, our hearts content.

Stories Yet Untold

In the shadows, tales reside,
Whispers echo, secrets hide.
Every heart a world unique,
Every glance a story's peak.

Footsteps soft on ancient stone,
Lives unfurling, not alone.
Echoes linger in the breeze,
In moments paused, we seek to seize.

Pages waiting, ink runs dry,
For a voice that dares to fly.
Through the silence, truth unfolds,
In the quiet, life beholds.

Unwritten lines in the night,
Dreams igniting with the light.
Let us pen what time constrains,
In the stories, joy remains.

Treading on Moonlight

Beneath the glow of silver beams,
We dance along the flow of dreams.
Each footfall soft on starlit ground,
A symphony of night's sweet sound.

The whispers of the twilight sing,
Inviting hopes on gentle wings.
With every step, the heart takes flight,
As we tread on strands of light.

The night unfolds with every sway,
A canvas where we long to play.
In the shadows, secrets gleam,
Treading softly through the dream.

So let us wander hand in hand,
In the magic of this land.
For every moment, pure and bright,
Is found in treading on moonlight.

Echoes of the Unseen

Whispers in the shadows creep,
Voices that the silence keep.
Fleeting thoughts that softly sway,
Guiding where the lost hearts stray.

Glances cast at empty space,
Memories that time can't erase.
In the quiet, stories speak,
Hidden truths that seek the weak.

Ripples dance on water's skin,
Tracing paths where dreams begin.
Each breath carries tales untold,
Echoes of the brave and bold.

In the dark, they find their glow,
Silent paths we long to know.
Embers flicker, softly gleam,
Echoes weave the timeless dream.

Lanterns in the Mist

Softly glowing, lanterns bright,
Piercing through the veil of night.
Floating luminous and free,
Guiding souls like ships at sea.

Misty trails where shadows blend,
Searching for what lies ahead.
Each beacon, a whispered call,
A promise to not lose it all.

Underneath the haunted trees,
Lightness dances on the breeze.
Every flicker tells a tale,
Of the hearts that dare to sail.

As the fog begins to clear,
Lanterns glow, and dreams appear.
In the night, we find our way,
With lanterns guiding where we stray.

The First Breath of Night

As the sun dips low and sighs,
Stars awaken, fill the skies.
Moonlight drapes the world in grace,
A soft touch, a warm embrace.

Shadows stretch, then intertwine,
Crickets sing their lullabies.
Awakening the restless heart,
In the stillness, night imparts.

Night unfurls her velvet cloak,
In her presence, hush is spoke.
Every moment, time stands still,
As the world is lost in thrill.

Echoes of the day now fade,
In the calm, our dreams are laid.
The first breath of night arrives,
Carrying our hopes and lives.

Flickering Fantasies

In the shadow of the flame,
Whispers dance, they call your name.
Flickering across the night,
Chasing specters with delight.

Fractured dreams in fragile light,
Imagination takes its flight.
Every spark, a tale unique,
Voices of the bold and meek.

Painted skies and silhouettes,
Moments that the heart begets.
Fantasies in twilight's glow,
Showing all the paths we know.

As the embers start to fade,
Memories of light cascade.
In the dark, we weave our dreams,
Flickering in radiant beams.

Echoes of Unseen Journeys

In shadows deep where whispers dwell,
Footsteps trace a silent spell,
Faded paths of dreams untold,
Guide the wanderers brave and bold.

With every turn, a tale unfolds,
Of courage found and hearts of gold,
The distant call of ventures new,
Echoes sing of skies so blue.

Beneath the stars, the stories weave,
In night's embrace, we choose to believe,
That every journey has its grace,
Leading us to our destined place.

So take a step, let silence speak,
In every heart, a truth we seek,
For in the echoes, we reside,
In unseen journeys, side by side.

The Birth of Hope

In the dawn's soft, tender light,
New dreams emerge, taking flight,
A spark ignites within the soul,
As shadows fade, we feel whole.

Each heartbeat whispers tales of old,
Of love anew, of courage bold,
In every sigh, the promise grows,
A river flows where hope bestows.

Through tears we've shed and battles fought,
Resilience blooms in lessons taught,
With every step, we rise again,
In the birth of hope, there's no end.

Embrace the light, let spirits soar,
In unity, we seek for more,
For in our hearts, a flame will gleam,
The birth of hope, our shared dream.

Mirages of the Heart

In sandy dunes, the visions sway,
Fleeting dreams that come to play,
Whispers soft like desert winds,
Where reality and longing blend.

Through shimmering heat, the shadows hide,
Each wish a tide, a rising ride,
In the stillness, secrets dwell,
Mirages cast a mystic spell.

Yet in this dance of light and shade,
A deeper truth cannot evade,
What appears may not be fate,
But in our hearts, we resonate.

So trust the whispers of your soul,
For mirages guide to a greater goal,
In every illusion, a lesson learned,
A journey to where the heart has yearned.

Starlit Pathways

Beneath the canvas of the night,
Glows the world in twinkling light,
Each star a guide, a wish, a dream,
Together forging a silver seam.

Across the dark, our steps align,
In harmony, our hopes entwine,
Through cosmic lanes of endless skies,
We chase the glow where magic lies.

With every breath, the universe sings,
Of love and peace that starlight brings,
As constellations weave their grace,
We find our strength in this embrace.

So walk upon these starlit ways,
Let dreams ignite in bright arrays,
For in the night, we find our way,
Starlit pathways guide our stay.

Essence of the Unwritten

In whispers soft, dreams take flight,
Unseen stories bathe in light.
Through spaces where silence breathes,
Unwritten tales weave as they please.

Fragments dance in the twilight air,
Voices echo, emotions bare.
A canvas pure, yet undefined,
In every heart, the truth aligned.

Words unsaid linger in thoughts,
Embracing hopes that time begot.
Eager minds in stillness trace,
Stories waiting to embrace.

Canvas of the Unimaginable

Colors swirl in dreams once known,
Imprints of life, seeds are sown.
On canvases that waver and shift,
A world awaits our playful gift.

Brushstrokes dance with endless grace,
Imagined realms, a vivid space.
Where visions bloom like fragrant flowers,
Each stroke of fate unveils our powers.

Unseen hues blend in soft embrace,
Whispered tales in time and place.
In each creation, magic lies,
Born from the heart, beneath the skies.

The Spark in the Shadows

In corners dim, a flicker glows,
Beneath the veil where no one goes.
Whispers murmur what should be,
A spark ignites, wild and free.

Fleeting dreams in hidden nights,
Ignite the dark with secret lights.
In stillness lies a fervent plea,
To find what waits, to just believe.

The spark in shadows, a guiding flame,
Shaping destinies, calling names.
In every heart, that ember grows,
A truth unveiled in silent throes.

Transcendence in the Stillness

In moments quiet, worlds unfold,
Beyond the rush, treasures untold.
In the hush, a heartbeat's song,
Transcendence whispers, life is long.

Still waters reflect the skies,
In tranquil depths, the spirit flies.
Each breath a step beyond the noise,
In silence dwells the purest joys.

Amidst the calm, we learn to feel,
The universe in every reel.
Through stillness, rise, embrace the day,
Transcend your fears, let hope lead the way.

Fragile Flickers of Enlightenment

In the quiet dawn of thought,
Ideas dance like candlelight.
Flickers soft, yet so profound,
Whispers of truth take flight.

Chasing shadows, minds set free,
In the maze of dreams we roam.
Each spark ignites a path unseen,
Leading us toward our home.

Fragile threads of wisdom weave,
Nature's secrets to unfold.
In stillness, we learn to hear,
The stories yet untold.

Awakened minds begin to soar,
With hearts aglow, we seek the new.
Fragile flickers guide us forth,
In every thought, a breakthrough.

A Journey through the Ether

Whispers travel through the air,
Across the vast, uncharted sea.
Boundless realms of light await,
Inviting souls to wander free.

Stars like lanterns in the night,
Illuminate the path ahead.
Each heartbeat echoes in the void,
A symphony of dreams unsaid.

With each step, horizons shift,
Time and space begin to blend.
The ether sings a timeless tune,
On this journey without end.

Through the waves of cosmic breath,
We find our place in endless sky.
A dance of worlds as we embrace,
The universe, you and I.

The Quest for Light

In the heart of darkness deep,
A flickering flame begins to rise.
The quest for light, a noble path,
Where shadows fade and hope complies.

Through valleys low and mountains high,
We search for glimmers, pure and bright.
In every corner, every heart,
The yearning beckons, seek the light.

With courage strong and spirits bold,
We journey forth, hand in hand.
For in the depths of every soul,
A spark of light is always planned.

As stars align and dreams unfold,
Together we shall find our way.
The quest for light, forevermore,
A promise kept, a dawning day.

Winds of Change

Gentle breezes kiss the trees,
A whisper past the old and new.
Winds of change, a constant force,
Remind us life is ever true.

With every gust, a story's told,
Of journeys taken, dreams refined.
The tides may shift, yet here we stand,
Embracing all that we can find.

Leaves may fall, but roots hold tight,
In cycles grand, we learn to grow.
Winds of change, both fierce and calm,
Guide our hearts where they must go.

So let them blow, these winds of fate,
With open arms we face the sky.
In every shift, a chance to rise,
To dance with change, to soar and fly.

Awash in Serendipity

In the breeze, sweet whispers play,
Finding joy in the light of day.
Chance encounters weave a song,
Leading hearts where they belong.

Every twist a gentle fate,
Moments shared, never late.
Laughter dances in the air,
Memories, treasures we all share.

Shadows fade as dreams unfold,
Stories ripe, waiting to be told.
Embrace the warmth as it arrives,
Awash in bliss, the spirit thrives.

Radiant Dawn

The horizon blushes bright and fair,
Gold and crimson fill the air.
Nature stirs from slumber deep,
Promising secrets to keep.

Birds awaken with morning's song,
In their chorus, we belong.
Sunlight spills on dew-kissed fields,
Gentle warmth, the heart it shields.

A canvas painted, fresh and bold,
A new day's story to be told.
With each ray, hope takes its flight,
Embracing all in morning's light.

Celestial Currents

Stars align in cosmic dance,
Whispers guide in silent trance.
Galaxies swirl with tales untold,
In the night, dreams unfold.

Comets race through velvet skies,
Illuminating wandering eyes.
Every twinkle, a path anew,
Connecting hearts in the vast blue.

Planets spin in rhythm's flow,
Waves of light that ebb and glow.
Cosmic forces pull and sway,
In celestial currents, we find our way.

Charting the Stars

Maps of silver across dark seas,
Guiding souls on whispered breeze.
Constellations, patterns bright,
Leading us through the endless night.

With each flicker, a wish is made,
In the stillness, fears do fade.
To wonder lost or found,
In the vastness, we're all bound.

We search for signs in endless blue,
Charting paths that feel so true.
In the cosmos, dreams take flight,
As we journey toward the light.

First Light of a New Dawn

A soft glow breaks the night,
Whispers of warmth take flight.
Promises in shades of gold,
Awakening dreams long told.

The stars begin to fade,
While shadows serenade.
Eyes open, hearts ignite,
In the embrace of morning light.

Birds chirp a sweet refrain,
Nature's song calls again.
The world reborn, it's true,
With each hue, a fresh view.

Hope dances in the air,
With every breath, we share.
Together we rise and dare,
To greet the dawn laid bare.

Beyond the Veil of Sleep

In dreams, we float on air,
Carried by silence rare.
A realm where shadows play,
And night gently slips away.

Whispers from the stars call,
Echoes that softly fall.
We wander through time's stream,
Chasing the edge of a dream.

Fleeting moments intertwined,
Fragments of life defined.
As dawn breaks through the mist,
Awake to what we've kissed.

The veil begins to lift,
Revealing nature's gift.
With eyes wide and hearts keen,
We embrace what's ever seen.

The Canvas of Possibility

A blank slate waits ahead,
Where colors blend and spread.
Each brushstroke tells a tale,
Of dreams that dare unveil.

Imagine worlds anew,
In hues of vibrant blue.
With every choice we make,
A masterpiece to awake.

Lines and curves intertwine,
Forming paths that brightly shine.
What once was but a thought,
Now dances, richly wrought.

Infinite dreams unfurl,
In this magical swirl.
Together we create,
A future bright, innate.

Unraveled Mysteries

In shadows, secrets lie,
Beneath the midnight sky.
Threads of fate entwined,
Whispers of what's confined.

With curious minds ablaze,
We uncover the hidden ways.
Each question sparks the flame,
A riddle yet unnamed.

Paths untraveled call our name,
As we embrace the game.
With every clue we find,
The fabric of truth unwinds.

So journey forth into the night,
With hearts as our guiding light.
Unraveled, we will stand,
Discovering mysteries so grand.

Whispers of Tomorrow

In shadows where dreams softly tread,
Hope dances lightly, never misled.
Stars twinkle in the silent night,
Guiding hearts with their gentle light.

Whispers linger upon the breeze,
Carrying tales that never cease.
Every heartbeat a step to take,
In the quiet, new paths to make.

Morning rises, casting away fears,
Gathering strength from joyous tears.
Each breath speaks of what's to come,
In the stillness, the promise hums.

With courage forged in the darkest days,
We chart our course in new, bright ways.
For tomorrow is a canvas wide,
Where our hopes and dreams abide.

The Dawn of Aspirations

As the sun breaks the horizon's grip,
A chorus sings, on a new day's trip.
With every ray, ambitions soar,
Casting shadows on the past's closed door.

Voices echo in the morning air,
Aspiration's fire ignites the care.
Hands reach out for the distant star,
Believing dreams aren't too far.

In the warmth of fresh beginnings,
Life awakens with joyful winnings.
Every moment holds a chance,
To join the world in a daring dance.

Breathless whispers of what's ahead,
Coloring the skies, our dreams are spread.
With each new dawn, we rise anew,
Filling our hearts with a vibrant hue.

Gateways to the Imagination

In the realm where thoughts take flight,
Gateways open, revealing light.
Colors swirl in a vibrant hue,
Crafting worlds both old and new.

Each doorway framed by hopes long sought,
Imagination spins a web of thought.
Whispers echo in the twilight air,
Inviting all to dream, to dare.

With every step, the unknown calls,
In this land where magic sprawls.
Through the portals, visions gleam,
We find ourselves in endless dream.

So take the leap, explore the scene,
Where dreams become what hearts have seen.
In this space, let your spirit roam,
For here, at last, you find your home.

Threads of Fantasy

Woven tightly, the fabric gleams,
Threads of color sewn from dreams.
Each stitch a wish, a silent prayer,
In a tapestry of hope laid bare.

Fantastical realms, both near and far,
Where the mind's eye sees each star.
Adventures spring from hearts unbound,
In every stitch, new joys are found.

Tales of wonder, magic's embrace,
Entwine our lives in a sacred space.
With every twist, the story flows,
Crafted from love, where fantasy grows.

So let us weave, with threads divine,
A world where dreams and hearts align.
For in the fabric, we find our place,
In the dance of life, we leave our trace.

The Silence of Anticipation

In shadows deep, the stillness waits,
A breath held tight, behind closed gates.
The ticking clock, a muted sound,
As dreams weave soft, in silence found.

The night is draped in whispered sighs,
Beneath the moon, the longing lies.
With every pulse, the heart will yearn,
For dawn to break, for chances turned.

Each moment dances, time crawls slow,
The fear of fate, the thrill of flow.
In quiet thoughts, the future gleams,
Awaits the light, ignites our dreams.

Horizons Unbound

The skies stretch wide, a canvas blue,
With golden rays that pierce right through.
Where mountains kiss the sunlit haze,
And valleys sing of endless days.

A whispering breeze, in tales it weaves,
Through fields of gold, where nature breathes.
With open hearts, we roam the land,
With every step, the world is grand.

The sea calls forth, in waves that swell,
To distant shores where dreams can dwell.
The horizon beckons, wide and bright,
Inviting souls to seek their light.

The Palette of Tomorrow

Colors burst in morning's grace,
On canvas wide, a painted space.
With strokes of hope, we dream anew,
In every hue, our visions grew.

The past may fade, but shades remain,
In every joy, in every pain.
With vibrant brush, we blend the day,
As futures spark and find their way.

A splash of red, for courage sought,
The green of growth, the lessons taught.
In twilight's glow, our stories blend,
A masterpiece, our hands must send.

Seeds of Inspiration

In quiet soil, dreams take their root,
With whispered hopes, they sprout and shoot.
Each seed a spark, a vision clear,
With love and care, we hold them near.

The sun bestows its warming light,
While rain unlocks the fate of flight.
With patience taught, the blooms arise,
Transforming ground to vivid skies.

Through storms, they'll bend, but not break free,
In every struggle, strength we see.
From fertile minds, new worlds will grow,
With hearts aligned, we sow and sow.

Journeys of the Soul

In the quiet of the night,
Wanderers roam the dream's light.
With each step, they find their way,
To a brighter, dawn-lit day.

Through valleys rich and mountains high,
They seek the truth beneath the sky.
With every heartbeat, every sigh,
The journey unfolds, spirits fly.

Past rivers deep and forests wide,
The soul knows paths it must abide.
In echoes soft, the whispers call,
For the spirit dances, free for all.

And when they find their destined shore,
They gather tales of ancient lore.
In the tapestry of life, they weave,
The journeys taken, dreams believed.

Whispers of Tomorrow

Beneath the stars, a voice is heard,
Soft and gentle, like a bird.
It speaks of hope, of dreams anew,
In the quiet night, it sings true.

With every dawn, the whispers rise,
Carrying words from beyond the skies.
They promise light, they promise peace,
In every heart, they seek release.

As shadows fade and daylight breaks,
The promise of tomorrow wakes.
With open arms, we chase the light,
Guided by whispers through the night.

And in that glow, we find our way,
With every moment, come what may.
The future calls, a sweet refrain,
In every joy, in every pain.

Seeds of Stardust

In the cradle of the night sky,
Stars ignite and softly sigh.
They sprinkle dreams on earth below,
Seeds of stardust, they softly sow.

With every twinkle, stories rise,
Of distant worlds, of ancient ties.
In every heart, a spark is found,
Echoes of magic all around.

We gather wishes, hopes so bright,
In the garden of celestial light.
Through time and space, they gently drift,
A cosmic dance, a timeless gift.

And as they bloom in hearts and minds,
The universe in us unwinds.
In every soul, the stardust glows,
A tapestry of dreams that grows.

Awakened Horizons

As the dawn spills light on the sea,
Horizons awaken, wild and free.
With every wave that kisses the shore,
New beginnings whisper, 'seek for more.'

In vibrant hues, the day conforms,
Bringing forth life in endless forms.
With open eyes, we watch and see,
The beauty that blooms eternally.

Mountains rise, and valleys breathe,
Each moment a gift, we must believe.
In the dance of light, shadows flee,
Awakening hearts, a symphony.

So take a step into the day,
Let the horizon guide your way.
Embrace the world, let your heart soar,
For awakened horizons promise more.

Moments on the Verge

On the cusp of dreams we tread,
Whispers of hope, softly said.
Time hangs still, a breath held tight,
In the twilight, we seek the light.

Choices linger, paths unfold,
Stories waiting to be told.
We stand poised, the future near,
Moments fleeting, yet so clear.

Fears and wishes intertwine,
In this realm where hearts align.
Each heartbeat a gentle cue,
Life's vast canvas waits for you.

In the pause before the leap,
Promises echo, dreams to keep.
Let the silence pave the way,
For the dawn of a new day.

The Dawn of Awareness

Awake to worlds that softly gleam,
In every shadow, a new dream.
Eyes wide open, hearts in tune,
Discovering truths beneath the moon.

Thoughts unravel, visions bloom,
In quiet moments, break the gloom.
The mind expands, horizons grow,
In light's embrace, we start to flow.

Senses sharpen, each breath feels bright,
Guided by intuition's light.
In stillness, find the strength to see,
The dawn of all that we can be.

With awareness, fears subside,
In this journey, we confide.
With every glance, new paths ignite,
A tapestry woven with pure insight.

The Prism of Potential

In fragments of light, dreams collide,
Refracting hope, we cannot hide.
Each hue a story yet to weave,
In the tapestry of what we believe.

Shadows dance with colors bright,
Possibilities in every sight.
From the dark, a spark can grow,
Transforming fears to a vibrant glow.

As we gather shards of grace,
Each moment we learn to embrace.
Nature's palette, wild and free,
Reflects the depth of you and me.

Through this lens, we find our way,
In the spectrum of today.
With open hearts, we shall embark,
To find our light within the dark.

Subtle Signs of Change

In the quiet, a shiver stirs,
Nature's whisper, soft as furs.
Leaves begin to blush and fall,
The wind carries a gentle call.

Moments shift like tides at sea,
In the stillness, we start to see.
Patterns woven, threads of fate,
Small details that resonate.

Each heartbeat a sign, we must heed,
In the cycle, we plant the seed.
Change is subtle, yet profound,
In the silence, answers found.

With every breath, we learn to trust,
In the coming, we must adjust.
For all things shift, evolve, and bend,
Embrace the flow, let it ascend.

Maps of the Uncharted

Beneath the stars, where shadows play,
The unknown path calls out to stray,
With compass lost and hearts afire,
We seek the dreams that never tire.

In mists of time, the trail is veiled,
Every whisper of winds unveiled,
The ink of fate on parchment old,
A story waiting to be told.

Through valleys deep and mountains high,
Each step reveals the open sky,
With every turn, a chance to find,
New worlds to capture in our mind.

So let us roam where none have gone,
To chase the dusk, to greet the dawn,
In every heartbeat, every glance,
Maps of the uncharted, we advance.

Mirrors of Potential

In every face, a story lies,
Reflecting dreams beneath the skies,
Potential blooms like flowers rare,
Each glance a chance, a breath of air.

We walk the lines of what could be,
In glimmers of possibility,
With every thought, a vision grows,
A seed of light that softly glows.

Through trials faced and battles won,
We find the power in the sun,
To rise like phoenix from the ash,
Embrace the moments, make them last.

For in our hearts, the mirrors shine,
With strength and hope, our spirits align,
In every whisper, every scream,
We hold the keys to all our dreams.

Songs of the Silent Sky

The moonlit night sings soft and low,
In shadows where the dreamers go,
Each star a note, a cosmic tune,
A serenade beneath the moon.

With gentle winds that carry sound,
In silent spaces, peace is found,
The universe in quiet sighs,
A melody that never dies.

Through twilight shades, where whispers dwell,
The stories of the heavens swell,
In every heartbeat, each divine,
The songs of night, like aged wine.

So pause awhile, let silence breathe,
In the stillness, we believe,
For in the dark, the light will rise,
With songs of hope from silent skies.

The Alchemy of Yesterdays

In moments lost to time's embrace,
We find the echoes of a face,
The chapters written, tales we weave,
In memories, we learn to believe.

From ashes past, the lessons flow,
A dance of sorrow, joy, and woe,
Each heartbeat marks a turn of fate,
In alchemy, we learn to wait.

Transforming pain to gleaming gold,
The stories of our lives unfold,
In every scar, a choice to rise,
A testament beneath the skies.

So gather close, the threads we share,
In unity, the burdens bear,
For in the past, our futures play,
The alchemy of yesterdays.

The Theater of Possibility

In shadows cast by hopes anew,
Dreams dance lightly, breaking through.
Each whisper holds a gentle thread,
Woven paths where hearts are led.

A curtain rises, spirits fly,
The stage is set beneath the sky.
In every gaze, potential gleams,
Life unfolds in vibrant dreams.

Voices echo, futures call,
In this space, we rise, we fall.
With courage strong, we take our place,
An endless tale, a boundless chase.

Together we create the scene,
And stitch the fabric of the unseen.
In this theater of maybes bright,
Awakening to endless light.

Glimmers of the Infinite

Stars do wink in velvet skies,
Each twinkle holds a soft surprise.
In night's embrace, secrets unfurl,
A cosmic dance, a timeless whirl.

Whispers stir the silent air,
Glimmers spark a fervent prayer.
In every heartbeat, worlds ignite,
Endless wonders take their flight.

Beneath the moon, dreams intertwine,
Echoes of the divine align.
In starlit thoughts, we softly sway,
As night beckons and calls to play.

Infinite stories, softly spun,
In every shadow, light has begun.
In this vast space, we seek, we find,
Eternity glimmers, heart intertwined.

Banners of the New Day

With dawn's first light, the day takes flight,
Banners wave in colors bright.
Hope arises with the sun's warm rays,
Guiding us through the morning haze.

Each moment brims with possibility,
As we embrace our shared reality.
Courage blooms where fears once lay,
Sowing seeds for a better way.

Voices rise in joyful song,
Unity where we all belong.
Together we stand, casting aside,
The weight of past, in joy we bide.

In every heart, a fire ignites,
Banners of dreams, a future bright.
We march ahead with spirits free,
Toward the horizon, our destiny.

In the Lull of Night

The world grows quiet, shadows creep,
In this stillness, secrets sleep.
A gentle hush, the stars awake,
In whispered tones, the heavens break.

Dreams drift softly on the breeze,
Carried far with effortless ease.
In moonlit paths, the heart can roam,
Finding solace, a peaceful home.

Beneath the cloak of twilight's grace,
We ponder life, we seek our place.
In every pause, the soul takes flight,
In the lull of the cozy night.

As dawn awaits beyond the dark,
Hope ignites, a fragile spark.
In this moment, we gently rest,
In the night's embrace, forever blessed.

Wanderlust Whispers

Soft winds call out in the night,
Guiding hearts toward distant light.
Mountains stand proud, oceans wide,
Adventure awaits, let dreams be our guide.

Stars twinkle bright, tales untold,
In every journey, a treasure to hold.
Paths not taken, places to roam,
With each step, we find our home.

Whispers of freedom, a sweet refrain,
Chasing horizons through joy and pain.
With backpacks full and spirits high,
We dance with the clouds, we soar with the sky.

In the echo of footsteps, a promise we keep,
Wanderlust whispers, waking from sleep.
Each moment alive, a canvas so vast,
Painting our stories, a legacy cast.

Footprints on the Edge of Dreams

On the edge of dreams, where shadows play,
Footprints linger, leading the way.
Each step a promise, a silent vow,
Fashioning futures, for here and now.

Moonlight dances on the dew-kissed grass,
Whispers of hopes, in night's gentle pass.
Every heartbeat, a story to tell,
In the realm of dreams, we rise, we dwell.

Through valleys of doubt, peaks of delight,
We chase the dawn, igniting the night.
In visions of gold, our spirits entwine,
Footprints on paths where our dreams align.

So take my hand, let's wander afar,
Together we'll navigate by the starlight's spar.
With each fading echo, our dreams will beam,
And leave behind footprints on the edge of dreams.

The Birth of Inspiration

In the quiet moments when stillness reigns,
Ideas blossom as the heart unchains.
Colors collide, a symphony starts,
The spark of creation ignites in our hearts.

Words tumble forth like petals in spring,
Whispers of wisdom, the muse takes wing.
In shadows of silence, voices arise,
Crafting our worlds beneath endless skies.

A brushstroke here, a melody there,
The birth of inspiration, dancing in air.
Chasing the echoes of thoughts yet to form,
In the storm of creation, our spirits are warm.

So let the ideas pour like rain from above,
Nurtured by passion, watered by love.
Inspiration awakens, a brilliant embrace,
Crafting our dreams in a timeless space.

The Sweet Surrender of Now

In the stillness, we find our peace,
Time slows down, our worries cease.
With open hearts, we gently flow,
In the sweet surrender of now we grow.

Moments unfold like petals in bloom,
Filling the air with a fragrant perfume.
Savoring laughter, the warmth of a smile,
In the essence of now, we linger awhile.

The past fades softly, the future unclear,
But in this instant, everything's near.
Each breath a treasure, each glance divine,
In the sweet surrender, we truly shine.

So take my hand, let's embrace the day,
In the moment's glow, we'll dance and sway.
For in this sweet now, our spirits unite,
A symphony of love, a canvas of light.

Bridges to the Beyond

In twilight's glow, the bridges sway,
Carving paths where dreams may play.
Across the mist, a whisper calls,
To hidden lands beyond the walls.

With every step, the echoes blend,
A journey where the soul can mend.
Old fears dissolve in amber light,
Towards horizons, bold and bright.

Each crossing leads to tales untold,
Of heart's adventures, brave and bold.
Embrace the unknown, take the leap,
For in the beyond, treasures seep.

Together we forge, hand in hand,
Bridges to realms, both vast and grand.
A dance of fate, a chance to see,
Beyond ourselves, who we can be.

Kaleidoscope of Desires

In vibrant hues, our wishes twine,
A tapestry where hopes align.
Each glance reveals a spark anew,
A kaleidoscope of dreams in view.

Yearning hearts in gentle sway,
Chasing shadows, come what may.
Fragments swirl, a colorful blend,
A vivid journey without end.

With every turn, perspectives change,
What seems distant can feel so strange.
Yet in this dance, we find our way,
A symphony of night and day.

Desires bloom like flowers bright,
In the garden of dreams, pure delight.
Together we learn, together we grow,
In the shimmering light, the truths we know.

The Garden of Potential

Among the seeds of futures sown,
A garden waits, where dreams are grown.
With every raindrop, life ignites,
Potential blooms in the starlit nights.

Roots run deep beneath the ground,
In silence, strength and hope abound.
Nurtured with care, through sun and shade,
The beauty thrives, each promise made.

The colors burst, a vibrant sight,
In every petal, stories light.
We tend the dreams we wish to keep,
In the heart's garden, secrets sleep.

Together, let our visions rise,
A tapestry beneath the skies.
For in this space, we come alive,
In the garden of potential, we thrive.

Shadows of Longing

In whispers soft, the shadows creep,
They hold the dreams we long to keep.
Silhouettes dance in twilight's glow,
A haunting touch of love we know.

Each heartbeat echoes, lost in time,
In tender moments, we find rhyme.
The longing lingers, bittersweet,
In quiet corners, where hearts meet.

Through veils of night, the memories play,
Each shadow speaks what words can't say.
We chase the echoes, searching deep,
In the stillness where wishes leap.

Yet in the dark, a light might break,
From shadows born, new paths we make.
For longing leads to love's embrace,
In every shadow, a sacred space.

Seeds of Enchantment

In whispers soft, the magic grows,
Tiny treasures beneath the snow.
With sunlight's kiss, they start to rise,
Awakening dreams beneath the skies.

Each petal's hue, a vibrant song,
Entwined in tales where joys belong.
Their essence swirls in gentle breeze,
As nature's heart begins to tease.

From earth to sky, the journey unfolds,
In every bud, a story told.
With care and love, these seeds ignite,
A dance of life, a pure delight.

So plant your hopes, let wonder bloom,
In gardens bright, dispelling gloom.
For in each seed, a spark divine,
Awaits the heart where dreams align.

The Spark of Possibility

A flicker glows in darkest night,
A promise wrapped in soft twilight.
With courage bold, the heart will soar,
Unlocking dreams and so much more.

Hope whispers low, yet strong and clear,
Embracing paths that once felt dear.
A journey waits, just take the leap,
In every step, the magic keeps.

Imagination lights the way,
Transforming night into the day.
With open mind and spirit free,
Life dances in possibility.

So chase the stars, let visions fly,
For within you, a spark can lie.
Embrace the journey, hear its call,
In every heartbeat, rise and fall.

In the Silence of Wishes

Beneath the stars, where dreams reside,
In quiet moments, hearts confide.
With every breath, a wish takes flight,
In the stillness, a guiding light.

The moon observes, a silent friend,
Listening close, as hopes ascend.
Each whisper held within the night,
A promise made, a soul's delight.

With starlit skies, the magic weaves,
In secret places, the heart believes.
In silence deep, the mind can roam,
Finding peace within its home.

So close your eyes, let silence sing,
In dreams bestowed, find everything.
For in the quiet, wishes bloom,
And life's sweet journey finds its room.

Lanterns in Twilight

As daylight fades, the lanterns gleam,
Casting shadows, a soft warm beam.
In twilight's hush, the world transforms,
Inviting peace where beauty swarms.

Each flicker tells a tale anew,
Of hope and joy, the heart stays true.
With every light, a story glows,
A bridge to dreams where magic flows.

The evening breeze whispers low,
As lanterns sway, their soft glow.
In this embrace, the spirit sings,
With open arms, the night brings wings.

So walk with me through paths of light,
In lanterns' dance, enshrined in night.
For in the twilight's gentle sigh,
We find our dreams beneath the sky.

Radiance in the Void

In the silence of the night,
Stars whisper dreams untold.
Colors dance in dark expanse,
Time's secrets unfold.

Waves of light gently surge,
Brushing shadows with grace.
Galaxies spin, a swirling blur,
In this vast, endless space.

Hopes rise like morning mist,
Filling the dusky air.
Each glimmer holds a promise,
A wish without a care.

From the void, a spark ignites,
A beacon shining bright.
In the cosmos, we find our way,
Radiance in the night.

Moonlit Pioneers

Underneath the silver glow,
Dreamers venture wide.
With the moon as guiding light,
They sail the starlit tide.

New horizons call their names,
Echoes in the dark.
Footsteps soft on ancient trails,
Each heart a daring spark.

Whispers of forgotten tales,
Linger in the breeze.
With courage wrapped in stardust,
They chase what makes them free.

In celestial winds they ride,
Pioneers of the night.
With the moon as their witness,
They journey towards the light.

The Cradle of Aspirations

In a garden softly grown,
Dreams take root and thrive.
Watered with hopes and wishes,
They flourish, come alive.

Beneath the sun's warm embrace,
New futures start to bloom.
Each petal a tender promise,
In this sacred room.

Stars twinkling in the night,
Guide hearts toward the sky.
In the cradle of aspirations,
We learn to reach and fly.

With every dawn that breaks,
Possibilities ignite.
In the sanctuary of dreams,
We rise with morning light.

Harvesting Light

Fields glisten with twilight dew,
As shadows stretch and blend.
Hands outstretched to gather dreams,
In this world we tend.

Sunlight dances on the leaves,
Whispering stories past.
Each ray a golden promise,
A memory to last.

Crops of joy begin to swell,
Beneath the shining skies.
We reap the bounty of our hopes,
As laughter never dies.

In every glimmer, we find grace,
With hearts open wide.
Harvesting the light we share,
Together, side by side.

To Dream in Colors

In twilight's glow, our visions bloom,
A canvas bright, dispelling gloom.
With each shade, a story we weave,
Colors dance, as hearts believe.

In whispers soft, the hues collide,
A symphony where dreams reside.
From azure skies to emerald seas,
We paint our hopes with gentle ease.

Amidst the stars, the palette spreads,
Infinite dreams in vibrant threads.
With every brush, new worlds appear,
In dreams of colors, we hold dear.

Through every stroke, our spirits rise,
In vibrant whispers, truth resides.
To dream in colors, bold and bright,
Is to embrace the endless night.

A Brush with the Future

With every stroke, the future calls,
A tapestry where fate enthralls.
In shades of hope and bright desires,
We paint our path, igniting fires.

The canvas stretches, wide and free,
What will unfold? What shall we see?
In visions bold, we dare to strive,
With brush in hand, we come alive.

Moments captured, time unwinds,
A brush with fate, where art binds.
Each color sings of tales untold,
The future waits for hearts so bold.

In silence, visions come to light,
A masterpiece born from the night.
With every splash, we craft our lore,
A brush with the future, forevermore.

Explorers of the Unseen

We wander paths, where shadows dwell,
With open minds, we weave our spell.
In whispers soft, the secrets hide,
Explorers of the unseen, we glide.

Through ancient woods, and skies so vast,
The echoes of time, we seek to grasp.
In twilight's cloak, our spirits soar,
Unlocking doors to realms galore.

With every step, the shadows play,
Invisible threads guide our way.
In the quiet hush, truth's light gleams,
We journey far, beneath our dreams.

In hearts we trust, as maps unfold,
The unseen whispers tales of old.
Explorers bold, we venture deep,
In every corner, secrets keep.

Writing the Unwritten

With ink in hand, we pen the void,
A tale of dreams, both bright and coyed.
Each letter formed, a journey starts,
Writing the unwritten, with our hearts.

In silent spaces, stories breathe,
In every word, our hopes we sheath.
With every line, a new path found,
A symphony of truths unbound.

Through pages blank, our spirits dance,
In every choice, we take a chance.
With timeless ink, we etch our fate,
Writing the unwritten, it cannot wait.

From whispered thoughts, to stories grand,
We carve the worlds with gentle hand.
In every book, a life explored,
In writing the unwritten, we are adored.